DEMETER

GOES

SKYDIVING

DEMETER GOES SKYDIVING

SUSAN McCASLIN

THE UNIVERSITY OF ALBERTA PRESS

Published by
The University of Alberta Press
Ring House 2
Edmonton, Alberta, Canada T6G 2E1

Library and Archives Canada Cataloguing in Publication

McCaslin, Susan, 1947-
Demeter goes skydiving / Susan McCaslin.

(Currents, a Canadian literature series)
Poems.
ISBN 978-0-88864-551-7

I. Title. II. Series: Currents (Edmonton, Alta.)

PS8575.C43D44 2011 C811'.54 C2010-908139-0

First edition, first printing, 2011. Printed and bound in Canada by Houghton Boston Printers, Saskatoon, Saskatchewan. Copyediting and Proofreading by Peter Midgley.

A volume in (cuRRents), a Canadian literature series. Jonathan Hart, series editor.

The University of Alberta Press is committed to protecting our natural environment. As part of our efforts, this book is printed on Enviro Paper: it contains 100% post-consumer recycled fibres and is acid- and chlorine-free.

The University of Alberta Press gratefully acknowledges the support received for its publishing program from The Canada Council for the Arts. The University of Alberta Press also gratefully acknowledges the financial support of the Government of Canada through the Book Publishing Industry Development Program (BPIDP) and from the Alberta Foundation for the Arts for its publishing activities.

Canada

Canada Council for the Arts Conseil des Arts du Canada

Alberta Foundation for the Arts

CONTENTS

DEMETER GOES SKYDIVING

So mighty was the mother's childless cry,
A cry that rang thro' Hades, Earth, and Heaven!
—Alfred Lord Tennyson

The mysteries remain,
I keep the same
cycle of seed-time
and of sun and rain;
Demeter in the grass
I multiply,
Renew and bless....
—H.D., from *Red Roses for Bronze*

The loss of the daughter to the mother, the mother to the daughter, is the essential female tragedy. We acknowledge Lear (father-daughter split), Hamlet (son and mother) and Oedipus (son and mother) as great embodiments of the human tragedy: but there is no presently enduring recognition of the mother-daughter passion and rupture.
—Adrienne Rich, from *Of Woman Born*

FOREWORD

What if Demeter, the timeless fertility goddess of ancient Greek myth, slipped through a crack into the twenty-first century, shook off her ankle bracelets, corn tassels, and garlands, and began a tour of our improbable culture? In tracing her tracks, I relied primarily on Helene P. Foley's translation of the Homeric *Hymn to Demeter*, a poem composed between 650–550 BCE, not by Homer, according to most scholars, but by an unknown bard of the oral tradition. Poets from Dante to Milton to Swinburne to Adrienne Rich, Margaret Atwood, and Louise Glück have explored the many variants of the Demeter-Persephone myth, as it is one of the most profound mythologems or traditional, archetypal narratives of the ancient world. The abduction of the Kore or maiden to the underworld by Hades is a construct embedded in the very matrix of our collective consciousness.

If Demeter and Persephone were to arrive at our malls and freeways, what would they perceive, what would they say, and how would they move to resist or transform our current malaise and hopelessness? Out of this question, a new Demeter and Persephone are born, rising mysteriously from the very bones of the earth to lead us where they will.

Susan McCaslin

INVOCATIONS

1 AN EPIGRAM FOR THE MUSES

They initiate the conversation
but seldom help you finish.

The staying power
and signature
are yours.

Sly aunts,
slightly wicked
hobo goddesses of lost things
from memory's scrap pile

drop in with a word of advice

then disappear
like mice.

2 MUSE/MUSIC

What is the Muse?
            (music

Wherefore the Muse?
            (leagues and leagues under

Why the Muse?
            (joy of deep surrender

Whence the Muse?
            (a shipwreck

In what mode the Muse?
            (hibiscus in her arms

How the Muse?
            (by synapse

Wherefore the Muse
            (for nothing

Who is the Muse?
            (the parts of yourself thrown overboard

How the Muse?
            (no one afloat on another's anguish

Sweet remembrance?
            (remember sweetie,
                        one does not interrogate the Muse

DEMETER GOES SKYDIVING

to get an aerial view of the sucking terrain
where earth gaped and devoured her daughter.
She glimpses the iron-walled, underground mall,
its gates, trendy shops, thinning hype,
the Armani machismo of its Overlord,
politico, numb, sprawled in his corporate death.

Arms akimbo, she freefalls, wearing out gravity,
head over splayed feet tumbling absurdly through space,
plummeting, eyes half-closed, wincing almost
as she awaits the jerk of the tightening cords,
the chute that will or will not catch her.

She could call on Cupid or a sylph, no doubt,
but doesn't, though wind tears her cornsilk hair.
Crazy kamikaze void of music; her body,
unstately skywriting limned on Zeus's vault,
as if anything mattered after the wasting of her child.

She spells across the heavens, "Womb ache."
A slam poem slaps into the ground that is herself, Enna,
while her lost one puzzles over the seeds of a pomegranate,
all that she will allow herself in the bed of the dark king

who likes his women lean in their brief resistance.

DEMETER AND HEKATE DO LUNCH AT THE SAVOY GRILL

Two old dolls pencil a date in their planners:
she, of the wheat-coloured hair,
the other of the rippling, black coils, grey-laced.

Deme:
[Pushing a Kalamata olive around the plate]
Everyone's saying she might as well make the best of it
  down there.
After all, he's rich, drives a gold Hummer, and has relatives
  in high places,
but I say, what hope is there for a marriage that began with rape?
Now everyone's dressing it up as sweet persuasion, rapture,
  romance.

Kate:
What can you expect? They dubbed me a double-toil-and-trouble
mentor to witches, tricked me out an underground whore,
I, who lifted the marriage torches
and babysat the world's grief.

Deme:
Her shriek, you heard it pierce.
Now it has raised a porous pavilion in my bones,
a grave, unadorned site of rocking.
I have glommed onto zones of elsewhere.
Not present to myself or to the place where I stand,
I no longer heft the dream of earth in my hands,
or raise desire's seed, or feel the fertile swelling of the land.

Kate:
Two middle-aged women, practically invisible
who once had knee-buckling power.
Gentle words, wise words, harsh dollops of invective,
nothing gets through to the press.

Deme:
Blame it on the mothers. Too clingy.
All the experts do.

Kate:
Let's share this overcoat and head out in the rain,
fitting footfall to our shrugged-off lamentation.

PLUTO FAILS TO EVISCERATE HIMSELF OF DESPAIR

How to cleanse miasma hovering in his gut?
Only extending control gives relief
and the daily operations of the Corporation he bent
  himself for,
his empire of strip malls virulent in Tartarus and beyond.

(Maybe he'll trade his dreadlocks for a buzz cut this year.)

He chews his lip, taking stock of this slip of a girl
who once was Spring and now is clearly turf.
Fashion mogul, high priest of the runways,
he preps her for the catwalk decked in next year's trends.
String bikini, sash slung low, implants riding high.
Sunken cheeks, caved spine.
Keep them thin and weak.
Let them perfect the stiletto mince.
Call them Queenie and tell them they are empowered
in their self-immolation.
Avoid discourse

till they too embrace with unquestioning hunger
their assured self-commoditization.

HADES' GYM

When he tires of dispensing pharmaceuticals
(Effexer/elixir, Paxil/peace pill,
Prozac/Muzak, Celexa for Alexa),

he self-medicates by hanging out at his gym
over the door of which posters blare:
"Don't Wait for the Grim Reaper,
Run Yourself Into the Ground Now."

"Control is Pleasure."
"Addiction, the Happy Affliction."

Teens and pensioners pound their heels
on the fluorescent-lit treadmills of the dank underground,
trying to work up a sweat under posters of Sisyphus.

"I must, I must, increase my bust"
shoots from the mouths of anorexic grandmas,
a sad plainsong, all the poetry they know

in the land of the depressing dumps,
this glut of naught
and poppy seed croissants.

Persephone, with a bump in her tummy,
does lunges, counts off a hundred sit-ups on the ball,
stares into the mirror on the wall.

Multi-tasking is a breeze.
Read about all the subterranean stars
(who's fat, who's thin, who's out, who's in).

"While pounding the StairMaster, nothing's a disaster."

The hungry ones outside the gate,
the bombed-on shrieking children blown sky high,

can all be muffled for the buff at heart.

PERSEPHONE IN HADES

Awake as one dead among the dead,
I hear voices whisper I look pale
and inquire if I've been ill.

Some do not see me at all.
Some shudder and turn.
The snow is a crust I cannot consume.

I walk in my own tracks
past curbside detritus—
melancholic meanderings.

There is no regret,
though neighbours stare
at the nameless wraith

and thrust in my hair
their querulous glances.
Yet I to myself am solid

as dice thrown by the wayside.
Feet like roots walking,
a churning aimlessness.

Only Cerberus, curious, sniffs my fingers.

DEMETER, GRIEVING, AVOIDS GRAINS

celiac goddess of cereals,
serial killer of her own wan hope.

Each day she wakes to stone ingrown to heart,
no movement, desire, disclosure,

just a thin veil of frozen tears
springing behind the eyes.

Gaia's floor, a network of ice where no rose
mars the monochrome

now that Demeter bars all blooming.

Photosynthesis is dis-invented,
and the seasonal rotation stalls.

All purple crocuses withdraw into the gap
where delicate ankles vanished.

Again, a sharp *akhos*, grieving, hits the heart
and in that fissure she wanders the world,

each day a year, nine years, nine days
allergic to herself, ambrosial grain.

How to keep lamentation within bounds
is not the core question

when breath centres on Kore's melancholic throne.

DEMETER TRIES TO ADOPT

My daughter's crowning head was a midden of matted hair
neither light nor dark, her arms a cornstalk folded round her body,
hidden gold, first bloom holding shades of deeper bloom

(a procession of footfalls among hyacinth).

In the Mysteries, they would call this an unveiling,
such a simple thing—
singular ear of corn, sheath of wheat on a table.

When I laid her on my breast, no one, not god or *daimon*,
nor my own premonitory voices whispered:
"Contain this joy. Prepare for loss."

Milk and tenderness brought her almost to puberty;
yet the menstrual blood had not flowed
before the gods of culture clutched at her dress, chanting:

You are never good enough.
Glut yourself but never be satisfied.
Be the best you can be in everything all the time.

No letting down.
Languor is laziness.
We live on a dying planet your ancestors have gutted.

Consume. Consume.

So when the Assailant arrived, she put up but feeble resistance.
Now, lips pressed, I lave another woman's child in seasoned fire,
seeing ebullient in flame my own dear melancholic's face

though love has altered and a fissure opened in the heart
depositing a stone.

WAS SHE FORCED TO EAT THE POMEGRANATE SEEDS?

or did she of her own volition?
Both.

Seeds flaunted like labels in a red Gucci bag
must be desired, must be
coveted when living enchantments
drain from the clouds and tender faces of flowers.

Come buy, come buy!

Was she tricked?
Did Hades waft them under her nose,
tracking the REM pattern of her eyes
on a screen showing lit neurons firing in her head
while she was lucid dreaming?

Did he chant softly in her ear,
"Shop till you drop to save Avernus"?

Why so alluring, these small seeds?
Did they promise undulations of lover and beloved
she had imagined before being swept into a world
with no within?

If so, no such *hieros gamos*
issued from the abyss of their centre.

Did they mirror the arrested flow of her menses
or the brief narcotic still life
of a world devoid of birds?

Whatever lay in the balance,
the vermilion fruit glowing on its stem
would never be the same.

DEMETER, DROWNING, REMEMBERS A LOVER OF HER YOUTH

Demeter flails,
having lost sight of the beach

with its small breathing holes for crabs,
the figure eights of tides,

dance of kelp-drawn lines.
Breath folds,

arms, weakening tentacles.

Soon she will relive
the blue-black flanks of Poseidon

who harried her once,
became half-stallion for her sake.

Now she is a single spar,
dragged to his Sargasso eye,

lone witness to her self-abandonment.

DEMETER SPEAKS TRUTH TO THE POWERS

1

I became a wordless, dour wrath
pausing only briefly at wells,
wandering dust storm whorled away

where I knew myself as bond and disjunction,
booty and bride,
bearing within both mother and daughter

(a grain of wheat falling into the earth).

2

You, Greed-barons, with your poisons, tanks and wars
delving and dredging my fields,
you lied when you said how Hermes led her up,

for it was I who trod layers of detritus and sludge,
upturning amphora, column, frieze,
descending deeper and deeper

into the dark excavations of the self,
till I came at last to the seat of violation,
mindless ripping asunder of clods,

unholy rites, stripping of slopes,
all the vast planet stretched
scarred beneath my feet.

3

I have torn the garlands from my hair
to declare here a dreadful peace,
demanding back the children

who have been given data
instead of meaning,
acquisition in place of a household.

PERSEPHONE STANDS STALLED BEFORE THE SHRINE OF CATHERINE OF SIENA

the instruments of self-flagellation, the account
of her final self-starvation.

Stench of sanctity appalls:
embalmed skull, relic of her diminution,

no larger than a three-year-old child's.

"Holy Anorexic," they named you,
wizened, wiser now?

And Holy you are and were and are to be
in word and text,

but unholy, unholy the culture
that urged this self-effacement,

abasement, erasure of flesh
your sole path to purity.

You who were clean and fresh
as first narcissus in a field,

not vain, but veined
with green causeways of our mother,

white stem and branch of our mutual source,
Mater Gaia, she who emerged from Chaos

overturning sleep to make us well.

PERSEPHONE SITS IN THE SILENCE

Stars long blotted
prickle the lids of her inner eye

(starry host, arranging itself there).

Sheaves of grain dancing,
imagery she dismisses with a wave,

consenting to deeper dark,
siren songs sinking to humus.

Now the conjugal embrace,
not to Plutonian realms

or to their shadow Lord,
or to reunion with all the anguishing mothers—

Cybele, Demeter, Hekate—
but to her own seed self,

as of a pomegranate,
oval in the heart.

Now a doubling,
mother/daughter; daughter/mother;

child in mother; mother in child.
Double Persephone; double Demeter.

Here just the scent of pine,
anniversary of the crowning of her own voice.

PERSEPHONE TOURS THE UNDERGROUND

on Hermes' electric golf cart,
zooms through dropping corridors,
past flinching factories, stifling cells
where skeletal children sew
designer emblems day and night
on the jeans of privileged teens,

witnessing how the upper world
rests on the muscle of billions below,
how the cosmos has become a pyramid scheme,
not the circular dream of Eleusis,
how here, even fireflies shed their luminescence
and no light blesses tortured, bloodied heads,

how the somnolent stumble on zigzag trails,
lugging poisoned water in pails,
how to reign as Hades' Queen is to lurch
with the uncountable destitute
under ignorant, affluent feet, (the uneasy gambit
of those above who have seen, considered
and turned away).

PERSEPHONE HEARS A LAYERED SINGING

Flanked by milling shoppers
jockeying for positions in line ups,
I walk through a labyrinthine, underground mall,
past elegant makeup counters, robotic joggers,
into rooms of stockpiled merchandise,
oil tanks, missiles, endless silent hallways

that open at last on a corn-yellow room
where light streams from a skylight
on the braided head of a woman
playing a grand piano and singing.

She is not young or old, familiar or unfamiliar,
but has the timbre of one who had been my mother,
one long thought dead.

And what a voice, as of all octaves slung together,
an Ella voice, a rich contralto hymning "Summertime,"
voice broken and repaired in each measure,
voice beyond control and controlling
voice of longing and release
voice of resisting and yielding,
voice making no division
between upper and lower worlds,

liminal, liberating voice without score
no ulterior motive but to sing
the song which is the world
in all its rich atonalities, lifts and falls.

(For if one can so sing, anything may be possible.)

So this is how I come to the upper world,
not shoving one foot before the other,
but remaining where I am and rising on a voice.

Often now, I am in the deep underground
and simultaneously above,
being both spring and winter,
all seasons rotating together.

HADES FORWARDS HIS CASE

It isn't as if I chose this
mask of bad guys everywhere,
a sort of Darth Vader grin.

Call me Augustus, Napoleon, Bush I or II,
if the sceptre fits.
But consider being a kid

dominated by an older brother all those years,
who after stealing the inheritance,
sets himself up on the hill

with servants, posh food, armies,
then (feigning generosity)
hands me this underground hovel,

magnificent through I've made it,
decked out like the city of Venice
with chipped, plaster facades,

a whore outlasting too many fetes.
Well, I've made the best of it.
And it isn't easy patching together

some kind of male identity in these times.
Guys have issues with food and exercise too.
It isn't as if I'm abusive or behind the times.

Women down here have had the vote for years,
and lots of them are lawyers, doctors.
So when Zeus proposed marriage with his daughter

to kind of consolidate relations,
who was I to say no?
Now the kid ignores me,

disappears for weeks,
wants to go home to her mother.
What do you think that does to the old male ego?

So I keep oiling the machinery,
testing the bombs,
keeping the place safe for her and all the dead,

in case she comes back.

UNDERGROUND OLYMPICS

Picnickers recline on the green at the edge of the abyss,
a grassy slope for the fashionable luncheon crowd
whose pineapples slide off toothpicks amidst martini chatter,
where fine-pressed olive oils ooze, and canapés
rotate on trays, a plenum of organics.

Beyond the polished green where groupies lounge,
a pit of spikes and pinnacles arises,
heart-tearing terrain over which the athletes,
pumped and psyched, soon will scrabble,
puncturing their adamantine knees on the escarpment.

This is a course they have circuited
marathon after marathon, almost grazing
with their hands the ribbons and the fountains,
accolades coveted from afar with glittering eyes.
And, make no mistake, they will beat

not just their own time, but everyone else's,
for these are the dead heroes torqued by Furies,
their own relentless nightmares, flicking
flies from their fabulous flesh, surpassing jets
in the need to rip the laurel from someone else's head.

Here at the starting line, they twist and jibe,
while those who raptly view the spectacle,
the ironclad elite, aficionados of perfection,
kneel on the slopes, fresh from hours
in traffic jams or stuffed in Metros, Tubes.

With Stygian tides, dissatisfactions unstemmed,
they fling themselves
again and again
into virtual space,

this brief and heavy catharsis.

DEMETER PAUSES AT THE FOOT OF THE KOKANEE GLACIER

So far west, past prairies
into avalanche fields that swallow children whole

into thrusting breaths of purest air
where for a nanosecond sorrow lifts

like cloudcover, unveiling acres of rock
where even old Thunderfinger cannot penetrate,

deep into the ground of an interior weeping
that makes the bluest blue of lakes.

Here, the wide-eyed anemone flaunts,
fireweed flames past fear of being plucked.

This time the goddess does not compromise
but surrenders her fertility to snowfields

singing, I am She,
Isis gathering dismemberment in her arms,

Mary weeping at the foot of the cross,
all wandering, grieving mothers

brought to prescience in my body.
I am She, sleeves of silver flashing over the Slocan.

Part of my daughter is beside me now
and part of her is out of reach

though nothing is unto itself enough
in these alpine floral sprays.

WHY DID I EAT THE POMEGRANATE?

Each day a different answer
falls from another chamber.
Mostly I think it was the allergens:
first meat, then dairy, white sugar, rice and bread,
grain in all its mucilaginous mass,
the curling up embarrassment of wheat.

Ruby gems gave an illusion of food,
unreal tang, promising satiety.
Now I mouth the names of the dead
who like syllables troop before me,
bartering for blood, wages of loss,
hoping to grasp the voluptuous in my shade.

I have watched the young soldiers arm themselves and fall,
but the wars against the self are the most terrible.

Humans could have crept out of the earth
unaccompanied by such beauty—

violet streaks of the pansy,
brushed against the wing of butterfly's gold—

thrusting its fragility, even here.

DEMETER'S RAGE

Heaving mother, mater out of stone,
where corn shivers,
drops contract into themselves
fast in the fist of the sun.

You will not turn the seasons' wheel
or lift the body's heavy semaphore,
and even Gaia shrugs off your tumult,
tunes to that older song—"Endure."

Yet all the livid, ashen mothers,
present, past and future, press
in one volcanic rush,
slam vases, pots and glasses at the wall.

And out the door surge all the stunning ones,
Aphrodite, Artemis, Hebe, stunned,
lust, love, virginity arm in arm—
a vast progress of rage.

DEMETER WANDERS THE GLOBE

Grief-embedded

like a journalist in a foreign land,
how could she have known

till she closed her eyes nine days
and plunged in double dark,

wandered in the wheezing gulfs of war,
that the one who seized her child

was not god or man, but an estate,
a state, a citizenship,

a culture seizuring,
dipped in bronze, warriored,

prinked out in mind metals
with all its wealth clamped down,

a vectoring that would tamp
the throat of irises

and lock them in cabinets;
and that a culture bound

to such proud perfectings
would petrify, make flawless falls

of ice, a rimmed cutting off,

screeds of greed;

and that the ripening ones
could live here only briefly

and queendom would be a rule
over dead ones only.

RUMOUR'S HEYDAY

Some say Hades transmogrified
into a good but gloomy mate,
that he and the young woman
consummated their lust,
and she ate the fruit,
not because he tricked or forced her,
but because their pornographic nights
were truly filmworthy

and the Mona Lisa glances she bestowed on him
betrayed a goddess smitten;
that Zeus and the boys
had worked it all out beforehand,
and Hades was not such a bad match after all.

This at least was the version they fed her mother,
the lie of Helios who witnessed the violence,
hiding the irony of Kore's cry to her father Zeus,
who (unbeknownst to her)
arranged and condoned the whole thing,
then insisted the ending made it not so bad:
part of the year with the mom,
the rest in the bed of the god,

a workable compromise with patriarchy.
And not even a single lawyer's fee.

(But none of this is so.)

For all the time,
Persephone was searching for Dionysus—
a god of whom there are few accounts
of his having raped a woman,
though he did drive a few Maenads crazy,
(but that wasn't his fault).

She fancied a man who would fill the house with flowers,
not those boring asphodels, but jasmine, lilies, roses,
distil pinot noir,
sleep all night in the arms of the earth.

DEMETER LAUGHS

I, Iambe, old serving woman,
claim honour from the gods
for making the post-menopausal Demeter guffaw.

With one risqué joke, a lifting of my skirts,
she who had been silent, veiled,
refusing to quaff my herbal brew,
suddenly felt mirth rising from her left side,
a swelling from the basement of the belly,
staccatoing through the chambers of her chest.

First a titter, then a giggle,
passed from gut to brain
to heart, to lung, to eye to feet,
a cavorting roundelay
converting the whole household
to taboo-breaking rebirth.

Laughter sang in her
(definitely post-hormonal)
through dense dark

till she fell off her stool,
and all the long-gripped fury
leaked through the interstices of the room

and she, a goddess in hiding,
could not cup the explosion
or in any way contain it.

DEMETER OPENS THE MYSTERIES

Deo
closes her eyes.

Anterior mystic,
sinks into the black boggy din

and opens them again to mystery—
a shimmering sheaf of grain in Stygian gloom.

She would re-enact this closing
and lifting of the eyes,

this falling open of the mouth,
dropping of the jaw.

She would teach by being,
and so become initiate

in her own first rites
of re-enchantment,

proving in her body
how the three worlds are one.

GREAT-GRANDMOTHER STEPS IN

"Tell us what you want," Gaia said,
"A pleasure without pain," Persephone said,
and Gaia said, "No."

(Then the young woman realized
this wasn't what she really wanted.)

So she swallowed
the entire pomegranate,
seed, casement, juice and all

and crowned herself
Queen of contraries,
till what she had always desired

became her intent:
the power to move freely
on the stairway between worlds,

mind no more a barrier reef
to her most nuanced longing.
A fullness fully distinguished,

but not entirely separate
from that of her mother.

A balance within her
she could count on.

DEMETER HAS A SHORT COLLOQUY WITH HER INNER GAIA

D: Inside or outside?

G: *Both*

D: Mother or daughter?

G: *Both*

D: Pilgrimage or marriage?

G: *Both*

D: Festival or funeral?

G: *Both*

D: Resting or moving?

G: *Both*

G: What do you want, then?

D: *The heart, dear craft, not untimely ripped*
from the Mother
but sailing out of its own accord

A NUDE DEMETER DESCENDING A STAIRWAY

Though they said
Hermes played psychopomp,
it was Demeter who descended that moving stair,
escalator into Erebus, Styx burning below.

And the mother, joying in the daughter,
did not lead her up,
but the two women ascended side by side,
silent in the stultifying air

two women cascading though space and time,
above them little luminescent moons,
the alphabets of golden sheaves of wheat
folded over their arms.

DEMETER COMMITS OSMOSIS WITH THE BLACK MADONNA OF RUSSIA

You, Lady, sheathed in sorrows,
black and comely as Lebanon,
ebon icon of carved lids
and the tender inward-outward gaze,
cheek caressing your child,

curled chrysalis, awakening
who has not known bone-ache,
division, but is
nonetheless known.

Words whirl about the chamber,
letters zigzagging,
names colliding
in this brief epistle:

Dearest poet,

whose name is attar poured out,
grant me this day your daily child,
the young woman your womb wrapped

and I will grant you a poem's
peace slid under the door
on violet air, fresh
from my good dark

and besides, the spangled ah's,
                the aha's,
                                the long-drawn ooo's

in weltering silence

PERSEPHONE FINDS RUTH ON THE THRESHING FLOOR

Remember Ruth,
that Moabite maid, pagan,
who trudged with her mother-in-law Naomi to Israel
and would not be parted from her,

whose woman-to-woman plea,
no, assertion,
became a model for our wedding vows?

> *Wherever you go, I will go.*
> *Your people will be my people,*
> *and your God, my God.*

That night on the threshing floor,
when Ruth crept up to her kinsman Boaz's mat,

Persephone, Queen of the Dead,
dripping with golden gleanings,
whispered into her ear:

> *Flirt.*
> *Make heart-choice.*
> *Be pastoral.*
> *Sing:*
>
> > *"I am Ruth, ruthless.*
> > *You will spread open your robe*
> > *redressing a rapine not your own*
> > *with loving kindness."*

And out of that night flew Jesse, and David,
and the numberless unnamed daughters.

DEMETER IN IRAQ

Though my element is sod,
I crave the feel of flying now,
sharp churnings of the air,
                                        pivot and fall.

The plane drops me in the desert
where civilization began,
where I wander over blistering dunes.

Hades' troops precede me,
flinging fire into the night sky,
keeping surveillance.

Boys, beardless as Hermes,
blow themselves up for Allah—
dark alembics thrown.

I covenant with widows
and children in shuddering hovels,
slip in where sewage slides,

and slim Persephones
                                        (still, veiled)
cower in bunkers lighting weeping candles.

No red poppies decorate the ground,
only carmine flesh.

Sons, too soon soldiers,
burn to defy western lust for oil.

Blood of deep-veined Gaia,
hoarded so a remnant,
sick with excess,
can shelter from salt and bone
of the poor in spirit

who surely inherit my fields
and whom I freely bless
                                        and bless.

HADES TRAFFICS IN CORN

Demeter catches Hades on her turf
trafficking in corn,
his microscope honed on a seed,
encoding its rich innards.

Mystery will not meander here,
nor will the slender stalk
unwind freely from strewn seed.

Terminator seeds, agriculture's neutron bombs,
genetically programmed for sterility,
creep across the Mexican border,
polluting ancient crops.

Her own refusal of all bloom
brought famine once,
but that was from a dull and biting grief.
Now she stands with campesinos,
forced to buy their corn from Uncle Sam.

Transnationals and governments
mass market, produce, process
her shining gown, her crown.

The upstart god Monsanto, Hades' pal,
patents the intricate DNA,
sells pesticide-resistant seeds to farmers
who get attached and fold, prices too high.

The obese rich,
the famine-stricken poor,
Janus-faced,
don't know how they are twinned.

DEMETER ASCENDS MOUNT NORMAN ON PENDER ISLAND, BRITISH COLUMBIA

She could have been dropped by helicopter,
but prefers to hike over potholes,

up switchbacks to the summit,
only 800 feet, but the highest peak on the island.

In the Mysteries,
a mystic comes with eyes closed,

and, later, mouth agape,
but here,

with islands stretched like whales' backs,
the slate sky pearlized,

to shut the eyes would be irreverent,
for the eye wants to linger along the strait,

pick out cormorants, wharves, ferries.
The eye is on vacation here,

back in the image-flow.

Islands sleep in earth's ear canal,
and Demeter, gazing, is mothered

in the Mother at last,
stepping up to the tectonic plates,

penless
before the great utterance.

DEMETER, BORED IN HER HOTEL ROOM, WATCHES *HIGH NOON*

We the people can always be manipulated to hate
some demonized other.
—Alicia Ostriker

1

She flings open the saloon doors of the entertainment unit,
and behold, the flat grey screen
where Gary Cooper saunters in
at the flick of a remote.

Gary is a classic,
as is the film,
reminding her of her son-in-law Hades
when they first met, him tipping his helmet
so gentlemanlike, as if to say,
"Howdy, Ma'am, I'll take good care of your little gal here."

2

The Argument:

It's Gary's wedding day and he's married a Quaker, Grace
Kelly (who in real life gave up Hollywood to be a real
Princess, married the Prince of Monaco, had daughters,
and died in a car wreck), but here she's just a peace-loving
Quaker with a forgettable name who had the bad luck to
marry a U.S. Marshal in a dusty western town. Now
Marshal Gary (Will in the film), has a blue eye, even in
black and white, and a slow gait, but you can see he's
all churned up inside because the bad guys he put in
prison way back when are coming in on the noon train (at
"high noon" to be exact), and he doesn't want to fight them

'cause he's a peace lov'n, law keeping man, with a new non-violent wife and all, but he knows he has to strap on his pistol 'cause the meanest bad guy of them all is coming just for him and to terrorize the town, and even though Gary's tough, and a good guy, you can see under the make up he's sweating it out. So he goes around town trying to round up a posse to help him gun down those snake-eyed killers, who love to kill just for the hell of it, but sadly, no one will help Gary in his hour of need, not his neighbours, not the churchgoers, not even his very best friend, just one drunk and one boy, but Gary says no to that kind of help. And all he wants is to saddle up and ride away, but we know he won't 'cause the town needs him and he just can't be a coward, so he'll face down those four nasty gunmen all by his lonesome 'cause that's what a brave man does, but just in case of the worst, he writes up his last "will" and testament (no pun intended), then watches his honey ride to the train station in a horse and buggy, since a Quaker can't abide a would-be killer, while the score keeps playing, "Do Not Forsake Me, Oh My Darling." Well, I'll spare you the build up, but Gary, as you might guess, kills two of those slimy bastards, and, glory be, at the very last moment when it's curtains for him, his little Quaker wife decides to stand by her man and guns down the third all by herself, leaving Gary to finish off the fourth and worst beautifully. Then he hugs his sweetie, tosses his tin star in the dust, and rides off with Grace into the sunset (with the score still playing "Do Not Forsake Me, Oh My Darling"), never to be violent again.

3

Demeter's eyes are moist
for she could almost love Gary
and his pretty little bride

and, Zeus knows,
she would have killed once herself
to save her own girl,

but reminds herself
Nero and Napoleon, Teddy Roosevelt
and George Bush

and every hero on the block
who clings to a weapon of mass destruction
loves this film too

and sees in Gary his own goodness reflected
as in a tin star.

DEMETER FLICKS THE REMOTE TO *EXTREME MAKEOVER* AND WRITES ABOUT IT LATER

Dearest Hekate,

These girls can't afford such treatment, so when the limo comes to sweep them away, instead of screaming like Persephone when Hades pitched her into his chariot, they squeal with delight like the pigs our Eleusinian men used to drive into the pits before the rites.

The surgeon is avuncular. He grasps the girl's "image issue" right away and marks the parts of the face that require emendation. A lift of the chin, a chiselling of the Latino-American nose. But not to worry, "We'll keep that ethnic flavour."

Each in turn bares her chest and he delivers his verdict without scorn: "Mere pippins, not perky enough, nipples too large." She lets him determine their new heft and he winks, "A nice surprise for hubby. Oh, and your stomach's as flaccid as a 60-year-old's. But not to fret, a tuck here, some liposuction there will do the trick."

She weeps a bit before the anaesthetic, but he, her chief comforter and knife, instils faith.

A month later, he unpeels tenderly the bandages from her revised chin and arched brow. Doctor and patient jig around the ward like newlyweds. She is Lazarus unbound.

She phones her family to say all is well, except all is not well till after the abrasives and acid washes for the acne, and collagen treatments for the lips, veneers for tarnished teeth, and laser eye surgery so she can toss the schoolmarm glasses. “And, oh my dear, 5' 4" and 155 pounds. What can I say?” He scribbles out a regime for fasting on meted fruit, veggies and protein—daily butt work at the gym.

At last, months later—the straightening of kinked hair, the designer gown, plunging neckline, scarlet heels, jewels, and, voila!, a new Aphrodite risen from the foam!

In the limo to the reunion, she is giddy and tearful. Assembled family and friends gasp as she pivots on the spiral stair. “I'm myself,” she beams, “only better.”

And her husband, who has been secretly indulging in tango lessons all these long months with a sexy senorita instructor just to surprise his wife, takes her hand, his eyes moist with renewed lust.

Such things are done on western shores.

Yours, sitting with the sorrow,

Deme

DEMETER TRIES TO ADOPT BRITNEY SPEARS

Britney, America's erstwhile darling
at twelve, now fodder for YouTube,
her half-life held in Pepsi ads.

Cornered by paparazzi, she swings
her bared bum out of cars
too late to avoid the crotch shot.

"Hit me baby one more time"
with your cameras
en route to the custody trial,
coon-ringed eyes veering away.

Too soon modified, mortified,
commoditized, too soon married,
lean, a fatty chomped by the machine,
you, no heavier than Venus in her prime,
you, of the infatuating perfumes
no one will buy.

They have ripped you apart like Orpheus
and your stripped fragments fly all over the web
where your shaven head still goes on singing.

So I'm swooping in for an aerial pickup,
nabbing you by taxi,
smuggling you out of rehab
for Paris, with or without the kids,
where we'll dance on Marc Chagall's ceilings
and I'll introduce you to his mystic bride,
and the fiercely flying animals

and you can lie on the beach with Reubens,
where the fans who gobbled you up like candy
can never mock you again
and you will be calmed,
if not wholly convinced,
of your own hidden wholeness.

HYMN FOR A TOXIC CULTURE

Grieve the crocus children, rose children,
they of the flowering faces,
narcissus wholly strewn, wholly broken.

Shun the compulsive march,
mother and maiden torn asunder.
Pity the duality kings in self-enclosed splendour.

Join the mothers, fathers
in the child-honouring dance,
join the creeping, crawling ones.

Join the cultivated and the wild,
the gazing grain
tall in the eye of the sun.

Join the pomegranate children,
garnet-coloured seeds spilling
from within, not rudely forced.

Join the swelling of the ground,
the descent in gossamer,
the chthonic mother's soft embrace.

DEMETER WORKS ON NON-ATTACHMENT

Steps out of "mother" into that which is.
Looks around.

The mind is winding up her puppets,
who bow and fret, swinging
their caps crazily to get her attention.

Aching mom. Self-tombed.
Dramaturgy of the soul
over Lotharios and deadbeat dads.

Too young, her darling shelters
in a tent of gloom. Gloomy queen.
Morpheus draws a sheet over her bed.

So Demeter steps further back,
past the teeth-grinding, lip-chewing
band of clowns that parade in her mind.

She even pities Pluto now,
whose name means wealth,
realm lush with glow worms and diamonds.
His eyes march past armouries
looking for what? Himself,
a boy who loved to gather leaves,
and gaze into mud puddles.

And stepping back even further
she hails the wide sweep of anointing stars,
eternity on their brow,
the twin hemispheres of the brain,
their endless conversation.

DEMETER, EXITING THE MOTHER ROLE, FALLS INTO PRESENCE

Farewell rounded breasts, milk-stained, held in an infant's clutch.
Farewell roundelays and rocking, rippling morning lullabies.
Farewell reassuring hands, guiding her first stumbling steps.
Farewell godspeeds to schools, culture's corridors and twists.
Farewell teeming adolescence, the slow construction of a self.
Farewell resistance and protection, the niggling fights and snares.
Farewell admonitions, anticipation of barriers and blackness.
Farewell holding and letting go, letting go and holding
into the deep relinquishment, icon of disappearing feet,
slender body tilting into the ragged, rifled earth.

Now her daughter will be dangerous, afloat, reckless, her own
verisimilitude, charm and plenum.

Demeter hovers in the abyss, face to face with the spaciousness
of her own silences.

DEMETER'S DRUM

As at Eleusis, Demeter begins
the old dance, the lifting of torches,

the waiting at crossways,
the hugging of the ground
where she is soft footfall, laughter,

tread to be taken up by the lame ones
who move into her circles,
planetary oasis, sway of tears,

a looping of blue threads,
hearts in hiding, hesitant dreamers,
who, reaching some critical mass,

land in Love
churning chaos,
               and then....

OLD LOVE

That is no country for old men. The young
In one another's arms, birds in the trees
—Those dying generations—at their song...
—W.B. Yeats, "Sailing to Byzantium"

ARCTIC SOPHIA

You are travelling through a landscape of ice fields, snow-covered mountains, and cerulean skies. Stretched before you are pools of glacial-blue intensity, some nestled into ice grottos and caves. Steam rises from the pools and they beckon from a distance—hot springs, geothermal dazzlers, warm eyes gazing up out of the white permafrost. A group of you, tourists and pilgrims, makes its way from a log lodge and hikes across the snowfields to the first of the hidden pools, where you strip off your heavy gear and plunge into its welcoming warmth, as at a resort or spa. You remove your backpack, parka, clothing, and boots and plunge in naked. The waters relax yet invigorate, melting away years of stress. After a day exploring a few more of these hot spring grottos, you re-dress and make your way back toward the lodge.

As you enter the building, you notice a side door that leads to a small room where it is whispered a wise woman is "telling fortunes." Curious, you wait in line for your turn to have a few words with the sage. Finally, you enter an unadorned room with no furnishings, nothing on the walls. At one end of the room you see a very aged woman lying on a pallet or stretcher on the floor. She seems to be dying; yet her eyes are the exact shade of blue as the Arctic pools. She is a living embodiment of the Arctic landscape, all white-headed but with eyes like sapphires. She signals you to kneel beside her bed and tell your story.

You pour out all your cares, relating how you have retired recently and feel a bit lost, uncertain whether to write another book, study French, offer a workshop on the mystics, or travel to Africa. You confess in tears how you are having trouble disentangling your life from that of your twenty-one-year-old daughter, and that you feel like a failure as a mother and a human being. Then you blurt out that you are also feeling your age—sixty-one—and have new aches and pains, the start of arthritis, a back problem, grey hairs at the temples.

Through all your babbling, she remains silent, absorbing, making a space for your confusion, shame, grief, and fear. You have never experienced such absolute, non-judgmental attention. Yet as you speak of aging, she quite unexpectedly throws back her head and erupts into a tsunami of laughter. At first, you're embarrassed, assuming she is laughing at you; then you realize how absurd it is that you should be telling this "Ancient of Days" how very old you feel. To her, you are a child. As you notice her creased face, the face of the oldest person you have ever seen, you grasp the absurdity of your whining and start to laugh too. Her laughter is infectious, a compelling outburst of sheer, unadulterated joy. Finally, you stop and wait for a word from her, your Sophia, Mother, friend. For you are suddenly aware this being before whom you are kneeling is absolute Being, Becoming, beyond all dualities, is God, is the whole of the wide universe, all that is, condensed into the form of an old woman. She has an androgynous quality, yet she is clearly feminine.

Then she leans toward you, grasps both your hands in hers, locks her eyes with yours, and enunciates clearly and slowly—"BE BOLD!" Bold! In that moment, a radiance plays in her face that makes her seem young, and you feel as if being bold is the most natural and easy thing in the world. The stretcher or death bed seems a maternity bed. There is no more for her to say or you to receive. You are dismissed. But you know what she has transmitted will remain, and that you will be pondering it for a long time. What does it mean for you, here, now? Bold. The short, crisp, almost masculine Saxon word contains the word *old* but is not limited by it. It is stark, a spitfire utterance reminding one of "Eric the Bold" or some Viking conqueror, but clearly applies to the spiritual realms. Or did she mean bold like the Arctic landscape itself, deep blue contrasted to gelid white. Or bold, like the opposites fire and ice, containing in themselves their opposites? Or bold like a mother who has cast off the kind of mothering you felt was expected of you for some new mode of being. Or bold like the Holy One who lies still and silent in limitation yet whose one small word pierces the heart and is somehow food for the journey? Through the encounter itself you are bolded. Time will unfold bold.

GAIA

When she first rolled out of herself
there was nothing,
just infinite folds of her own
humid flesh, diorama of a volcanic brain.

She attended an inner quickening,
pulse upstaging any Blitzkrieg
humans could devise, humans,
those delirious, unpredictable ones

she would later name "natals"—"born of woman."

Their impending chatter was nothing
to her uninterrupted eruptions,
firework festivals.

So she dandled Tyrannosaurus
on mountainous knees,
set him on a plain—
a mere smoothing of her lap.

Then she formed a crust sprouting
scarlet-scented leaves,
crocuses weeping dew.

They say Uranos, Starry Sky,
covered her in the thunder
of new roilings between them

but, in truth, she covered him
as he went under and down.

And though in their first orgasm
she saw the trenches, rapine, landmines,
sutures sewn millennia later in her ageless flesh,

she continued bearing children, undaunted
by all their armaments and Armageddons.

IMMAGINI DI PARADISO

An earthquake shatters the musty glass cabinets
of the ornithological museum in San Gimignano
and all the beautiful specimens,
extant and extinct, hoist their pinions and glide
into the blue gown of space
past the broken orifices of the frescoes—
Upupa epops, Berta minore, Cincia dal Culffo,

each lofted viol,
each Etruscan drum,
one only a thumb's breadth and length,
whirligigged into the possible present,

that only aperture

(aliens so familiar
our winglessness aches for their song).

OLD LOVE

Burning even yet,
the ancient one weeps into the fissures,
tracks and trestles of the brain,
lightened by gardenia's fragrant phrase,
older even than coupling earth and sky,
hatched question without amen—
such a dogged gentleness.
How old, old love,
from what abyss cast up?
The old in each other's arms,
mother dancing her calf,
tensile wing of eldest Erós,
dark in the mediate zone,
a voice like shale,
birthing a nautilus child,
slung in the slender femur
and breastbone of salvation.
The days of the avatars have passed,
for we are avatars all,
our small flames quickening.

Our small, quickening flames
when we shall all be avatars
and the days of the avatars have passed.
There is a breastbone of salvation,
life slung in the slender femur,
where nautilus child births
with a voice like shale,
dark in the mediate zone,
tensile wing of eldest Eros,
who dances her calf.
The old in each other's arms,

from the abyss cast up
from old, old Love,
a dogged gentleness,
hatched question without amen,
older than coupling earth and sky
lightened by gardenia's fragrant phrase,
tracks and trestles of the brain,
the ancient one weeping into fissures,
burning even yet.

TURTLE LOVE

He sidles up to her on the road.
Bang, bang, taste my fire.

She is armoured in her nunnery,
but her head swivels sideways.

Bang, bang, bang, he knocks.
She is indifferent to assault

and galumphs away;
He would be her Easy Rider,

cover her like the Bosphorus Strait.
He would take her head in his mouth,

though she might wrest it away.
Undaunted, he sneaks up from behind,

mounts. Shells clack.
Such nakedness lost

under so much outerwear.
Then, timeless rocking,

his spurting shrieks of pleasured pain.
Again, again,

while she absorbs
and cradles within herself

that ancient offering.

HOW TO LOVE AN OLD DOG WITHOUT ANTHROPOMORPHISM OR SENTIMENTALITY

Probably impossible.

But when you take him strolling,
let him linger at trees, posts, hydrants.

Don't jerk his head with the leash,
for he needs to absorb a world beyond your gaze.

Even with cataracts and ear fungus,
his senses are still a thousand times

more world-caressing than yours,
his adoration of the earth more earthy,

more enamoured of grittiness and scent.

Remember how as a pup he tugged
and you could not keep his pace?

Now you drag him away
from his slow digestion of the real.

Though he surpasses you in dog-years,
he has not tasted death

but worshipped all his life
at the shrine of the Mother.

Don't confuse anthropomorphizing
with conceding to him his passions.

Remember Descartes,
who insisted beasts knew no pain

though they howled on science's wrack.
Honour Pavlov's dogs

whose tests proved (as if we did not know it before),
how easily we can make mechanisms of ourselves.

GATINEAU PARABLE

Thou canst not more clearly approach to the likeness of the Infinite by being a human than by being an ant; not more nearly by being a star than by being a human.
—Giordano Bruno

Ants sculpt twin towers on the Gatineau trail.

A minuscule door opens at the apex
to admit scrambling sentinels.

Thud and thrum of my feet
fail to mar ziggurat towers of their making.

A few steps further, three mounds more

rise pyramidal, cupping pupae, larvae,
nectar, crumbs and pollen.

(No sirens shriek apocalypse.)

Archaic carpentry resumes,
as does my Sunday stroll

past beings fractal, fragile,
who at least do not bomb or undermine

their own perilous citadels,
holding unaccountably to their posts.

I HAVE HEARD THE COWS LOWING FOR THEIR CALVES

The first month in our rural home
a shrieking ruckus in the night
startles us from sleep.

Perhaps the cows wish to warn
of an impending storm,
maybe even an earthquake,

their disconsolate bellowing and baying
prolonged like Rachel's weeping
for her children who were not.

Next day, a neighbour says
this was just the keening of cows
for young untimely weaned

the bawling calves' sad repartee,
providing at last a sound
commensurate to my inward lamentation

for my own dear child.

NEXUS OF BLISS

What if instead of a net of complaints
we entered a nexus of bliss?

If we are constituted and composed
of woodbine and violet,
why such dimness? If even a dog
knows what's torn from time, this patient
peering by the fence as an ether falls, nosegay
of columbine, stairway of pine, delved
sod rich with garnet eyes, then
why don't we fall into the daily glory
instead of hitting and hitting
the sharp-edged reef of self?

              Once as a girl,
rather than conceiving a Being outside
(Cosmic Spy, Note taker),
I saw ash trees limned in green

walking, hallooing, testing the air
              on gold wings of a pharaoh's daughter.

MY MOTHER'S HANDS

One last look at my mother's rivering hands,
blue veins, swathed in skin's diaphanous caul.

Rings long removed
imprint a circular story of love, loss, love.

All unconsciously
she brushes aside a host of crumbs

unwitting etiquette,
even in propinquity of death.

COHORT OF SOLITUDE

Right in the midst of all this debacle
over wills, diminished estates,
bills, papers, intents and purposes,
sits my mother
            calm, breathing deeply as in a lava tube
where Presence exhales freely in her for the first time
since her girlhood in Alabama.

Now incontinent,
with papers rattling overhead, incognizant
of dwindling accounts, vertiginous
affairs, she murmurs
words of little consequence.

"Poor thing," relations say,
of she who drifts all day in Ra's sun boat
under the world
            where the carved paddle of her right eye
                        dips straight into mine,
casting my childhood name at my feet—
                        then back again to sleep.

My hand gentles her brow, sailing
through hulks of ruination.
A woman, fed, unwrapped, cracked
wracked and smiling.

Eye ventures into swift currents
then back to coverlets and fog.
No grimace,
just the sheer will
to paddle her wheelchair down hallways.

Unconscionable, to disturb such preparations,
Mysterium, where maps flail the air,
schedules singe, disintegrate.

Holy babble rolls deep,
proposition past crucible and forge.

THE LONELINESS OF OLD WOMEN

Like the second witch I played in Macbeth in Grade 7,
one twisted crone

crumples in her wheelchair, propped by the wall.

Another anorexic skeleton, all spine and skin,
coils in foetal posture.

One groans, another clutches at my coat.
Another, more observant, hoots,

"I'll bet you dyed that hair."
Then again, louder,

"No one your age has black hair, lady."

The cavernous spite of the aged,
or dementia, the lifting of all censors?

No wonder we parse our visits, check the clock,
slip quickly past those fingers that beckon,

"Come over, dear."

Their care home pabulum we decline and decline:
frozen peas, powdered potatoes, pan-fried breaded veal,
and custard.

"Thanks, but I've already eaten."

Their quick snatch-and-grab,
the moments of dignified silence or dark humming

when we wonder whether they are studying infinity,
or maybe absolute nothingness.

HOMING

Sometimes the unspeakable
bends and bows in our speech
honouring our heavy word platters

with wafers of light.

Sometimes the mysterious
cavern between my thighs
opens and we are both

found in that unknowing.

Sometimes, from way out there
the impossible waves its wand
and we are dragonflies floating home,

divinely accidental.

DREAM OF A BODHISATTVA

Outside the window a hurricane.
Ice storm rips the house from its foundation
plunging it in the sea, but the dreamer turns back
where a door leads to a conference room

containing Buddhists, Sikhs, Jews, Palestinians, Sufis,
acolytes, priests, nuns, adepts, seekers, gurus,
a table overflowing with melons, peaches,
and garlands festooning the walls,

air an embrace
against which there is no resistance.

Yet the dreamer resists, backs outside
throws herself into the vortex of the ice storm—
because there are locked doors, the poor at the portals
clawing—

too many left outside the circle.

THE GOSPEL OF MARY MAGDALENE

You are the light you have been moving towards,
said Mary, a woman of intimacies,
who spoke in silence an interior speaking,
high to low, in to out, leaf to branch.

Said Miriam, a woman of intimacies,
cored, yoked, interwoven with matter,
low to high, out to in, branch to leaf:
There is no sin in the waking world

for we are cored, yoked, interwoven with matter,
yet all that is composed shall be decomposed;
there is no sin in the waking world;
a babe strung in a hammock shoots into the night sky.

Yet all that is composed shall be decomposed.
So Peter and Andrew repudiated the woman's words,
while a babe in a hammock shot into the night sky
and emptied herself as from a tomb.

Peter and Andrew repudiated the woman's words,
whose hair swept by anointing stars,
who emptied herself as from a tomb
becoming awe and the fully human

whose hair swept by anointing stars,
who spoke in silence, an interior speaking,
becoming awe and the fully human:
You are the light you have been moving towards.

HALLOWEEN NIGHT ON SKYTRAIN

On the platform,
a jocular man sniggers—
his hectic grin and walnut eyes.
I inch away to join a safer group—
Draculas stomping in the cold.

Seated inside, I dissolve into Rilke's *Book of Hours*,
alternative inheritance, the wall between us so thin.

Just then, four voluptuous goddesses erupt through the door,
bared thighs resisting
germ-laden seats.

The most gorgeous, in sequined stilettos
and a Betty Boop skirt, looms over me,
the eyes of the druggy beside me,
staggering up and down the cheeks of her bum,
soon drop lost into Avernus.

Her sparking ruby slippers, unlike Dorothy's,
fail to click and lift her homeward.
No, she is, as she tells one inquirer,
a hairdresser, party bound on this night of all souls.

I could sing them these words:
My god is dark and like a web.
I've been circling for thousands of years—
    falcon, storm, or song?

But what are the words of an invisible middle-ager
along the fertile crescent of their track?

MAGDALENE

There are so many Marys
but this particular Mary
had a box of ointment very precious
an urn or amphora
inscribed with ancient characters
that was the interiority of Mary
and hers alone
nard, frankincense, attar of roses
and some mysterious, unidentifiable fragrance
that was the pure essence of Mary,
misnamed "sinner," lower than leper,
more salt than sea brine,
turbulent, broken cauldron
mended, rebroken.

And this Mary intruded, broke in
on the assembly of men and women
took up the urn like an udder of Nut, the starry sky,
and let it pour down over her own dark head
and the desiccated skins of the women with names,
Salome, Joanna, Susanna,
then at last
over the feet of Jesus, one among the women
who laid aside the shards
and knelt to massage Mary's feet,
and Mary smoothed his head with oil for burial and rebirth
till you could not say who was anointing
and who being anointed
who the Christ and who not the Christ
in the fragrance of the oil
which flowed over the lintel into the streets
and into the households of the poorest of the poor.

BORDER BOOGIE
(1969)

You who go out on schedule
to kill, do you know
there are eyes that watch you?
—Denise Levertov

1

Moon-pent in a white vw,
heading up the freeway north from Seattle,
sperm-like rain snaking up the windshield
toward Nirvana, British Columbia.

I am twenty-two
and deathless.

My boyfriend Tim and I slip
across the border just after Blaine
where he blew his mind on acid
a month ago on our first reconnaissance
of the route, hip, cool, tuned
to Coltrane's *A Love Supreme*.

2

The horrors of Hanoi,
napalm stuck in our skulls,
Levertov's logged words
encoding my journal.

Simon Fraser's radical curriculum
promises manna for the disenchanted,
tales of students storming the faculty lounge,
"Be-ins" for beleaguered flowering ones.

Tim drags along, averse to academics,
burying his letter from the draft board
deep in his duffle bag, moving
breathless past customs officials.

3

His dad chose for him a military career.
He told me how in officers' training
he leapt from a helicopter,
shot and skinned a rabbit, vomited,
then heaved himself out of there,

"tuned in, turned on, dropped out,"
found Monty his guru, and
a macrobiotic regime till I
caught him munching an Oh Henry!

Returning from a seminar on Blake
and the mythopoetic mind, I
became "The Little Girl Lost"
who found her lion deep

into Cream and Miles,
sprawled on the orange shag rug,
headphones riveted to his ears,
an astronaut trolling inner space,

splayed like Da Vinci's man,
skinny, open-faced.

4

He graduated (barely) in physics
but sought the Tao of imagination,

did piecework, house painting,
lineman jobs, stoned, toked up,

and with his first cheque bought me
a shimmering shift of red-orange glitter,
Aphrodite dress from a head shop.

He followed me to Vancouver,
pining for home, yet home meant

the draft and Vietnam,
hot killing fields and hollowed eyes.

5

Up all night typing papers on Poe's Berenice,
and Ligeia, I take to sporting dark capes,
grow pale with anemia,
believe that in another incarnation
I had been Poe's child wife Virginia Clemm.
(I always become what I research.)

My thesis grows pregnant with itself,
swells to 300 pages, mysterious,
white, like Moby Dick.

Tim, restless, disenchanted,
drives back and forth to Seattle.
We who had considered marriage,

split. I touch his head one last time
and choose to stay in Canada:
first hostel, hotel,
and finally, home.

6

Stuck with unknowing
all these years, I wonder:

Did he get snared by the draft?
Did he break and bleed in Southeast Asia?
Is his name inscribed on the wall in Washington?

Or is he a banker now,
easing into late mid-life
with a wife, a dog, and grandchildren on the way?

Googling gives no leads.
But who really needs to know?
The slide of sex, the glimmer gone,

all seems impossible, improbable
to my 60-something life.

Nevertheless, I would offer
more than ironies:
this last image of him falling

downstairs in a pool of his own light.

Errant knight,
held in a poem's peace.

A GLOSA FOR TONI ON HER SIXTIETH BIRTHDAY

Quiet friend who has come so far,
feel how your breathing makes more space around you.
Let this darkness be a bell tower
and you the bell. As you ring....
—Rainer Maria Rilke

After years of inspecting teeth,
gums' erosions, molars' chips,
the unflossed places where the floss Nazi
never comes, something inside you
turns, not knowing why, to another
profession, another form of attention. Like a jar
the hold of your spacious mind
cups all manner of folk, like us
who seek the pivot of your steady star,
quiet friend, who has come so far.

So you listen, making room for all sorts
of ragtag tales, sitting with fresh green grief
and loss, that dragonish weight, and darkness
of the body shedding time; then,
Eureka! Ecology and psychology wed
and you bring many to aurora-borealis dew
on wet cedars, opening the coffins of moths
spilling perfume of broken wings.
You teach them on island retreats to
feel how your breathing makes more space around you.

It's never simple venturing into the world.
Yet causes collect you, who serve them well.
This one and that, Mary and Martha twirled,
and all become another offered cup,
until the rhythm in and out compels
you to return to yourself some latent power,
the mystic life, a hidden poem rising
from fertile dark, the sweet transforming the sour:
Let this darkness be a bell tower.

Now on this fete-day of your sixtieth year,
we gather here to celebrate your being,
past, present, future, a unified display,
gentle original face within your faces.
A singer wants a partner, you with yours,
a sweet duet; add more to that—more sing.
Call it a quartet, it morphs into a choir;
a grand concerto plays in a grand hall.
Where voices dim and flare, you are the music's wing,
and you the bell. As you ring....

BELOVED, UNPARAPHRASABLE (30 YEARS)

You
homey pine
unrepeatable
scent broken-
open anthropos
engrained in
grizzlies'
grieving
a species you
utter lament for
unparaphrasable
spilling
(wildly) over
into me, un-
repeatably delicious
spelling
out, illuminated
alphabets
peer, peerless
companion, bread
breaker
boon-maker
beloved
unutterable
you

THIS WORLD IS STILL POSSIBLE

Where all the heroes have soft voices and weaponless hands
and the heads of corporations have broken their contracts
  with greed
and broken open their hearts to make stuff that matters
like caravans of oranges, mangoes, and apples flowing
to the poor who are bearing them in baskets to the poorer
and trickle down is a deluge for the common good
and everyone is greeting the Christ or Buddha in everyone
and the cruise missiles are being melted into serviceable tools
and the bombs' dismantling makes a postmodern music
and no bullets flail the air and no child stumbles on a land mine
and steeples of prayer deck the air with peace songs
and the professors become doers and transformers
and the dumpers of refuse in outer space become house cleaners
and girls are fed images of healthy bodies
rather than the airbrushed waifs of the media
and we make amends to the lab rats for Descartes
and young women run in back lanes without fear of being raped
and the disarmed heart of all hearts slowly lowers into the chest
and the whole magnificent household declares amnesty to the earth

TOGETHER, WE ARE RAIN (A VANCOUVER POEM)

Rain I, you, we, it, she, us: rain rimes rhythmic, arrhythmic,
precipitous rushing.

Aquatically-challenged cousin Fred said if we moved to the
wet coast we would
acclimatize to such alluvial aquatics, and like ducks, grow
moss on our backs.

It was so. Soon submerged in soggy, sumptuous rainforest drizzle,
interior arteries become aqueducts for rainfalls of green frogs.
It was us. We were rain and rain was us. We poured
ourselves out and spilled over.

Not that this was unpleasant. We adapted, noting that
being porous and permeable,
notwithstanding drenching, has definite advantages. One
can seep into a lover, fall
near like dew, transform from dew to ice, then on a whim,
nodding,
navigate rivers of bright sun and become a curtain of
golden rain.
Numinous, our circular cycle from cumulous, to deluge,
to rising mist is us.

Runnels and rivulets of us seek together some common source.
Rain invents in dialogue with sun the multiple names of green.
Rain reigns in Cascadia; let Montana weep if it can.
Rain in this bioregion grows cleansing tears.
Rain splashes on whales' heads and the roots of thirsty
  hydrangeas.
Rain ripples and runs like a renegade while California covets
  our water.
Rain pauses for breath, and the sun, valued tenfold, dances.
Rainmakers, rain dancers in Arizona, dream of us as heaven.

EARTH AS IT IS

As above, so below.
But it is not so, no.

Instead the muck-brown river,
sacked vault of heaven

and ourselves vandals
razing ancestral groves

the great alcove
imagined out there

beyond lunar satellites
interstellar voids

rather than within
ourselves, thought's other side,

an opening, maybe here
beneath fermenting blackberries

touchable delectation,
heaven still stabled, lodged, as it is.

EROS THE GREATER

You come shining between the line and its shadow
till there is no line, just swift trembling un-demarcation

suspending nothing from nothing where
forms emerge, float, separate reform, merge.

You fashion words' fallings and vanishings.
Such gallant regenerative generosity.

You, compiler, record keeper, scribe,
washing out mishap, mistake.

Such a wild one.

Nonetheless, not the lesser or petulant eros,
but Eros the Greater who rules by imagining

more, ever.
Such a crazy soul friend

amatory apostle of winds,
one galloping gesture

invisibly solid.
Impoverished god

gone wanting in the world
which needs dollops of you.

Now this is precise praise,
making all your worshippers one.

ARCTIC ARTICULATIONS

1

Sophia Wisdom falls into an orbit,
Orion Nebula in her arms,

drawing blue skirts around her thighs,
vortexing into arctic wind

to become ice floe, eyes
fluttering open as geothermal pools:

sapphire twins.

2

I walk into a long white room,
outside of which everything is melting.

The elder in the far corner lies afloat
in her armchair or divan

stretching her timeless limbs:
Well well, she says, *so what's the desire of your heart?*

3

I moan about how I'm getting older,
swollen finger joints carpal tunnelling
around greying temples, collagen-deprived
skin-boat capsizing on uncertain seas.

4

"Ancient of Nights, dear
Grandmother of grandmothers," I ask,
"Why these howls, chuckles, guffaws from your lips?"

Why, simply that my own Chaplinesque child
grumbles about her mere
half-marathon of days.

5

Next—if one can say "next" in such a place—
some temporal ripping occurs.

Aquatic eyes
restore themselves to piercing love-design.

6

Some words for me at last arrive:

a phrase, a trace
held out in shining script
cut from a dancing alphabet:

Be bold!

7

"Sophia,
Is this permission, admonition, licence,

or just time to step off
precipices

feeling held?"

CORONA ANNIVERSAIRE

(for Mark)

1

Take from my hands these sonnets, subtle nets
filtering the form of my desire for you
which grows secretly, somewhat reclusive,
then, surprisingly, pokes out its buried head
like a full term babe's and flings its voice
over mountains, calling you home, singing
our bodies' lift into vowels and music's
string of sapphires across Grouse,
moonrise, mosquitoes, consolation
of your moving limbs in sleep, so when
I slide into loss, you rise with touch,
kind words, and a cherishing of the tiny
hummingbird whose emerald breast
wheels at our feeder—graceful Arcadian.

2

Graceful Arcadian who wheels at our feeder
spins in with Gabriel's "Hail, Mary,"
dervish grace, whooshing into emerald
space, salvific fire, fitting the bowl of your hand,
cup of your eye. The motion
that is your body's morphic field
knows no disconnect from your face
of twenty-one years; so higher than altitude,
wider than panorama, we name the nearby
mountain, not "Golden Ears," but "Woman
with Knees Raised, Voluptuous in Birthing"—
so many animals sounding their small drums
from her wide womb, no prison house,
but ample with rivers and ruins.

3

Ample with rivers and ruins,
earth's womb breeds, space opens, cracks,
and in the crevice, a cave for a child—
she who comes forth clinging, leaving,
such a wonder in her athlete's gear,
running shoes, a new Atalanta for the race,
hair streaming in the fierce air,
damped only by our starvation culture,
though bull-like in her stance,
no one could have imagined her clear eyes,
the rattle of thunder on her lips,
the double helix weaving her difference,
the tenderness and pain of our letting go,
or the trust of such inconceivable conceiving.

4

Conceiving, we could not have conceived
such harsh schooling for our child, and for us,
so much heart-hail in one year.
Yet language in her brow, her tongue
touching and tasting everything, everything
utters, "Consume, be amused, buy, produce,"
till she thinks her shape not perfect enough,
and coats her lips with cherry-gloss,
inedible fruit—then grows meagre,
a shadow maiden, objectified virgin of the ads,
tossed on the reefs of adolescence.
A new kind of fasting whittles down her sainthood,
making her judge and compare against plastic,
while we her parents, wooing sleep, weep on our bed.

5

We her parents, wooing sleep, weep on our bed,
condemned to insomnia, wracked disbelief,
while you, dear husband, gentle warrior,
lover of creek, stream, and silent pool,
descend the stair, stripping yourself
of honours at every step, lower and lower
till a tape set off in your brain
erases the good words "love" and "dignity,"
and rains down hammers: "fail," "disconsolate."
You hoist your cross, swallow gall,
trudge to the wild—a numbness freezes your spine.
Only the memory of our singing flesh,
the way our sinking seeks our rising up
binds you on the wheel of the world's dark night.

6

Bound on the wheel of the world's dark night,
hurtling into naked, stuttering dark,
we are separate, each floating on a chaotic stream.
We enrol our small names in the one book,
then nameless, toil at cross purposes,
uncrowning our heads, terrorized by the severity
of the judges, the impotence of our good intent,
you, facing a host of hostile fathers,
I, a crazed mother's last descent.
Protection gone, some promises undone,
we change our names and addresses,
wash our hands, and mourn,
knowing that after twenty-five years,
we'll ride on, assuming nothing, everything.

7

We'll ride on, assuming nothing, everything—
and hope what rises will be new
like the variations of spilled sunsets,
the vast soul of our aging dog,
that all composted vegetation, broken junk
might be of use, folded back into the field,
that she who comes forth a young woman
will stumble frettingly into her cosmos,
that reeling stones, houses, gardens, doors,
will contain pauses, that there will be more and more kisses,
though the broken ground of these words
is far too coarse a net in which to catch
the form of my desire. Still—
take from my hands these sonnets, subtle nets.

NOTES

DEMETER GOES SKYDIVING

Enna: A field in Italy where, according to Ovid, Persephone was abducted. The locale is used again by Milton in *Paradise Lost* where he compares Persephone to Eve.
Pomegranate seeds: The fruit Persephone ate in the underworld. The act of doing so requires her to return there for half of the year.

DEMETER AND HEKATE DO LUNCH AT THE SAVOY GRILL

Hekate: (or Hecate) In the Homeric Hymn, Hekate, chthonic goddess of the crossways and of night, is Demeter's friend who helps her search for the lost Persephone and eventually serves as her chief attendant in the underworld. In later times she was associated with witchcraft and evil, but was originally an ancient goddess of healing.

PLUTO FAILS TO EVISCERATE HIMSELF OF DESPAIR

Tartarus: A deep, gloomy region of the Greek underworld or Hades, associated with torture and suffering.

HADES' GYM

Effexor, Paxil, Celexa: Antidepressants.

PERSEPHONE IN HADES

Cerberus: The three-headed dog that guards the gates of the underworld; hound of hell or Hades.

DEMETER, GRIEVING, AVOIDS GRAINS

Celiac: One with a sensitivity to gluten, a protein found in many grains.
Kore: "Maiden," the generic name for Persephone before she becomes Hades' wife and Queen of the Underworld.

WAS SHE FORCED TO EAT THE POMEGRANATE SEEDS?

Avernus (or Averno): Ancient name for a crater near Cumae, Italy, believed to be the entrance to the underworld; an alternate name for the underworld.
***hieros gamos*:** Sacred union, marriage, coupling; sometimes enacted between two gods or a god and priestess.

DEMETER, DROWNING, REMEMBERS A LOVER OF HER YOUTH

half-stallion: There is a legend that Demeter was raped by Poseidon in the form of a stallion.

PERSEPHONE STANDS STALLED BEFORE THE SHRINE OF CATHERINE OF SIENA

Catherine of Siena: Patron saint of Italy; Christian mystic (1347–1380).
narcissus: The distractingly beautiful white flower Persephone was reaching for when she was seized by Hades.

PERSEPHONE SITS IN THE SILENCE

Cybele: Ancient Phrygian mother goddess associated with Rhea and Demeter.

DEMETER PAUSES AT THE FOOT OF THE KOKANEE GLACIER

Thunderfinger: Zeus, as god of thunder and lightning.
Isis: Egyptian goddess, wife and sister of Osiris who searched the world for the dismembered pieces of his body.

DEMETER'S RAGE

Artemis: Goddess of the hunt, wild animals, and childbirth.
Hebe: Goddess of youth; daughter of Zeus and Hera.

DEMETER WANDERS THE GLOBE

nine days: The period during which Demeter roamed the earth fasting, searching for her daughter.

RUMOUR'S HEYDAY

Dionysus: God of wine and inspired madness or ecstasy; lord of the vine; some versions of the myth associate him with Demeter and Persephone. In one version he is Persephone's son, Iakkhos.
Maenads: Inspired, frenzied women who worshipped Dionysus.

DEMETER LAUGHS

Iambe: Also called Baubo; an old woman at the court of Queen Metaneira in Eleusis who made Demeter laugh with her ribald humour. In one version she raises her skirts and reveals her genitals to make the goddess laugh and break her fast.

DEMETER OPENS THE MYSTERIES

Deo: A shortened form of the name "Demeter" used in *The Homeric Hymn to Demeter.*
Stygian: Of or pertaining to the River Styx, the murky underworld river over which the souls of the dead must be ferried; infernal.

A NUDE DEMETER DESCENDING A STAIRWAY

Psychopomp: Guide of souls; one who escorts the newly dead to the underworld; one of Hermes' roles.

PERSEPHONE FINDS RUTH ON THE THRESHING FLOOR

Ruth and Naomi: Inspiration for this poem came from Alicia Ostriker's essay, "The Book of Ruth and the Love of the Land" in *For the Love of God: the Bible as an Open Book* (Rutgers University Press, 2007).

HADES TRAFFICS IN CORN

Monsanto: An American multinational agricultural corporation that has developed biotechnologies for making pesticide-free wheat.

Janus-faced: Roman god of doorways and gates with two faces looking in opposite directions.

DEMETER TRIES TO ADOPT BRITNEY SPEARS

Orpheus: Greek god who played the lyre, enchanting trees and animals, lost his bride Eurydice to the underworld, and was dismembered by the Maenad women, followers of Dionysus, though his head went on singing out to sea.

ACKNOWLEDGEMENTS

I wish to acknowledge the Canada Council for awarding me an Arts Grant for 2007–2008 in order to develop *Demeter Goes Skydiving.*

Much gratitude goes to poets David Zieroth, Alicia Ostriker, Hannah Main-Van der Kamp, Catherine Owen, Katerina Fretwell, and John Porter for their thoughtful responses to this manuscript in its various stages.

I also wish to thank my exceptional editor at the University of Alberta, Peter Midgley, for his care and attention to the manuscript throughout the editorial process. Thanks also to the dedicated staff at UAP: Cathie Crooks, Jeff Carpenter, and Mary Lou Roy.

Special thanks to my former colleagues at Douglas College whose retirement gift of a three-day retreat at a resort at Pender Island on the Gulf Islands in British Columbia allowed me to discover the cycle I considered finished was not yet complete.

And to the literary magazines and presses that first published the following:

"An Epigram for the Muses" in *Inviting the Incubus, Kissing the Succubus: the Muse in Canadian Women's Poetry,* Living Archives of the Feminist Caucus (League of Canadian Poets, 2005); and also in *Prism International* (Winter 2007).

"Demeter Goes Skydiving" in *The Silver Hammer Awards/ Anthology* (2007).

"Earth As It Is" in *PRECIPICE* (2007).

"The Gospel of Mary Magdalene" in *Arms Like Ladders: the Eloquent She, Poems from the Feminist Caucus,* ed. Katerina Fretwell, Living Archives of the Feminist Caucus (League of Canadian Poets, 2007).

"Pluto Forwards His Case" and "Persephone Tours the Underground" in *Ascent Aspirations Magazine: Anthology Five,* ed. David Foster (2008).

"Demeter Ascends Mount Norman on Pender Island, British Columbia" in *Rocksalt: an Anthology of Contemporary Poetry from British Columbia,* ed. Mona Fertig and Harold Rhenisch (Mother Tongue Publishing, 2008).

"Persephone Hears a Layered Singing" in *poetry strand,* ed. David Zieroth (Summer 2008).

"Magdalene" in *Ascent Aspiration Anthology,* Erotica Issue (2008).

"Immagini di Paradiso" in *Room: a space of your own* (Winter 2008).

"Homing" in *The Windsor Review* (Spring 2008).

"How to Love an Old Dog without Anthropomorphism or Sentimentality" in *Contemporary Verse 2* (2008).

"Border Boogie (1969)" in the anthology *Crossing Lines: Poets Who Came to Canada in the Vietnam War Era,* ed. Allan Briesmaster (Seraphim Editions, 2008).

"Halloween Night on SkyTrain," posted March 19, 2008, on http://blueskiespoetry.ca

A subset of poems from *Demeter Goes Skydiving* was first published in *Persephone Tours the Underground,* a limited edition chapbook (The Alfred Gustav Press, May 2009).

"Underground Olympics" in *Canadian Literature* (Autumn 2009).

"Together, We Are Rain (A Vancouver Poem)" was commissioned by Neil Weisensel, Music Minister at Canadian Memorial United Church in Vancouver, British Columbia, for a concert performed there on February 8, 2009.

"Demeter, Drowning, Remembers a Lover of Her Youth" in *Canadian Woman Studies* (Fall 2008/Winter 2009).

"Persephone Sits in the Silence" and "Rumour's Heyday," in *Contemporary Verse 2: At the Root of this Voice.* Vol. 32, No. 3 (Spring 2010).

A selection from *Demeter Goes Skydiving, in The Journal of Feminist Studies in Religion.* Vol. 26, No. 1 (Winter 2010).

"A Glosa for Toni on her Sixtieth Birthday" and "Together, We Are Rain (A Vancouver Poem)" in *Rhythm Poetry Magazine* (Fall/Winter 2010/Spring 2011). http://rhythmpoetrymagazine.english.dal.ca/i1v4/rhythm.html